Moonlight, Stuff and Nonsense

Moonlight, Stuff and Nonsense

Poems for the Reflective Years

C. W. Christian

authorHOUSE®

AuthorHouse™
1663 Liberty Drive
Bloomington, IN 47403
www.authorhouse.com
Phone: 1-800-839-8640

First published by AuthorHouse   07/05/2011

ISBN: 978-1-4634-1519-8 (sc)
ISBN: 978-1-4634-1924-0 (ebk)

Library of Congress Control Number: 2011909535

Printed in the United States of America

Any people depicted in stock imagery provided by Thinkstock are models, and such images are being used for illustrative purposes only.
Certain stock imagery © Thinkstock.

This book is printed on acid-free paper.

*To
Elizabeth,
Savannah, Sidney,
Eli, Ella*

and

their Aunt JoAnne

The majority of the poems in this little collection were written for the monthly Newsletter of the Baylor University Retired Professors/ Administrators Program, which program has been directed for many years by Dr. Rufus Spain. I wish to thank Dr. Spain for his support and encouragement in this project and the administration of a great university for sponsoring and underwriting this worthwhile organization. I thank also my many friends who have encouraged our efforts with love and appreciation. Above all, my thanks and love go to the lady who has been my steady presence for so long and who is the inspiration for not a few of the poems herein.

C. W. Christian.

CONTENTS

Confessions of a Doggerel Writer

When first I read that sonnet by the Bard—
"Shall I compare thee to a summer's day?"—
I started writing poetry by the yard,
Replete with every image and cliché.

Heeding my muse, it was my worthy goal
To let my spirit soar like Blake or Shelley,
To touch men's hearts or heal the broken soul.
Instead, I've prompted laughter in the belly.

Alas, the world has scorned me when I'm serious,
Ignored my pathos, overlooked my passion,
As if to say, "Your fulminations weary us.
Write us a poem in your foolish fashion."

And so I've smiled and donned Pagliacci's ruff,
I've worn the jester's jolly bells and sash,
And now I scribble volumes of such stuff
To make great Gilbert groan or Ogden Gnash.

But lest you think this destiny's appalling,
A giggle's not a bad thing to evoke.
So maybe this is still a noble calling.
Did Keats or Wordsworth ever crack a joke?

So I'll tuck my solemn stuff into the file
And ask the muse to bless my silly verse,
Hoping that I can make my readers smile.
There are, I guess, employments that are worse.

Confessions of a Polypassionist

(A sort of self-examination)

People there are who resonate to nothing.
Such persons are a mystery to me.
Some have a single, all-consuming passion,
A plague from which I've hitherto been free.

I am the fellow who is drawn to tears
By the unstained splendor of the midnight sky,
The drama of an autumn oak aflame,
The softness in a little daughter's eye.

Little there is of nature or of love,
Of artless gesture or of studied art,
That cannot reach my atavistic core.
I am a polypassionist at heart.

It seems to me if hearts were meant to beat,
Songs to be heard and beauty made for seeing
Then I can be forgiven if I seem
To feel with every fiber of my being.

If something in me is compelled to seize
On this dear world in part or in the whole
To dance or ache or laugh or weep or sing,
Then blame my polypassionistic soul.

Three Beasties

I

Praying Mantis

Hands folded in obeisant protocol
And full of piety as any tonsured monk
Or cloistered deaconess, his eyes cast down,
He meditates upon divinity,
Then seizes on a careless damselfly
Swift as an evil thought. He turns her once
And deftly snips her, abdomen from thorax,
Looking from side to side to ask
If his rapacity has been observed,
Calmly munches her still wriggling pieces
While yet he's saying grace.
Much of life's charm is incongruity.

II.

Squirrel on a Cable

As nimble as a circus acrobat
He'd walk the cable high above our fence,
Hurling squirrel invective at the cat,
Full of himself, his confidence immense.

There he would preen, until he failed to see
That day our local mockingbird set sail,
Like nemesis, swift from the tallest tree
To pound a tender spot beneath his tail.

Twenty feet straight downward to the grass!
Stunned but intact, he shook his small round head
And waited for the turbulence to pass,
But beneath his fur I'm sure his cheeks were red.

A time for due compassion, you'll agree.
I shamefully confess I laughed aloud.
What is it in my soul that joys to see
On any field the humbling of the proud?

III.

To a Grackle in Springtime

You strut across the newly-sprinkled grass
In glossy black and purple iridescence,
Dripping self-approval as you pass,
Lordly, amidst the sparrow peasants.

Extravagance of tail and glowing eye!
As vain as any peacock in Cashmere,
You point your shiny dagger at the sky.
No diffidence or due discretion here!

Where have I seen vainglory so secure
In anybody going. Tell me, bird,
As you parade in fatuous hauteur,
When does grandiloquence become absurd?

And what of your image when you deign to speak?
What can your khaki consort do but cringe
At what escapes your throat and quivering beak:
The vocal splendor of a rusty hinge!

Such profligate display would seem to be
Carrying self-regard beyond all reason.
And please don't flirt your sassy tail at me!
I've seen your naked rump in molting season.

"Play Ball"

(To my Dad)

Fast ball, slider, knuckler, curve—
Sweat and sinew, flesh and nerve.
Wind-up, pivot, heel and toe.
Keep it inside; keep it low

Fingers tight across the seams—
Still I do it in my dreams.
Still it echoes in my brain:
Summer sun and sudden rain.

Iron cleats in prairie soil,
Infield dust and neat's-foot oil.
Short-hop grounders in my glove,
Red earth beneath, blue sky above.

We were so innocent and chaste;
We played the game and then embraced
Before a hurting world grew mean
And drew a veil of spite between.

Youth and friendship, grass and sky.
A happy warrior once was I!
Helmet, saber, shield and buckler,
Fast ball, change-up, slider, knuckler.

First Steps

(Ella Josephine at One)

One foot affixed unsurely to the floor,
The other hovering doubtfully before,
She briefly contemplates the vision splendid,
Twixt stasis and mobility suspended,
Sworn to eschew her horizontal state,
Patently aflame to ambulate.

One tipsy lurch, another then, and three,
With countenance of pure, unzippered glee,
Triumph of the underling unfeigned,
Freedom dreamed of; freedom now attained,
Then settling for the safety of the chair.
But naïve, unsuspecting world—
Beware.

Son of Green Thumb

Mom was beloved of growing things,
A mistress of the blooms;
She'd stick a broomstick in the ground
And promptly harvest brooms.

I nurse my sprouts with loving care
Until they fairly smother,
But still they wilt with baleful eye
And whimper, "Where's your mother?"

Seventy-six Candles

How shall I observe the hour?
Six and seventy candlepower!
Of the century three-quarters;
Two of sons and two of daughters,
Little boys once shy and smiling,
Little girls demure, beguiling,
Children little, children grown,
Now with children of their own.
Past the measles, past pubescence,
Triumphed over adolescence,
Duly blessed with wisdom's charism,
Past the age when I embarrass 'em,
Mortal failings now allowed of me,
They even speak as if they're proud of me.
They bring their lively offspring now
To kiss me on my wrinkled brow.
Welcome, fateful natal day,
Six and seventy's Okay!

A Reluctant Aubade

The sky is red.
I greet it with a sigh
As on my bed
In lassitude I lie.

"Awake," you say,
"The moon and stars are gone!
Salute the day
And meet the glorious dawn!"

Just let me lie!
I'd rather not be rude
And stultify
Your beatific mood.

I greet the sun
Contentious and contrary
When roused by one
Intemperately merry.

You're right, I'm sure.
There's simply no disguising
The morning's lure,
The bliss of early rising.

But though I see
The snail that's on the thorn,
I'm doomed to be
Curmudgeon in the morn.

Rebuke me not!
The evidence is firm:
Consider what
Soon rising got the worm.

Tardy I crept
To bed, for slumber's sake!
Had I sooner slept
More blithely would I wake.

Desperation

Dearly beloved wife, beware!
Kindly unhand my favorite chair.

It would make my spirit weep
To see it on the garbage heap;
Threaten to discard no more
The furniture that I adore.
Ignore inconsequential things
Like shiny pile and sagging springs,
Like spots and stains we'll never clean
With Ajax or with gasoline.

Rather consider, if you will:
Its oaken frame is sturdy still.
And surely, Dear, you'll not ignore
How well it mellows our décor,
How it abets a morning nap,
A feline purring in my lap,
Or makes a winter evening cheerier
Snug around my plump posterior.

Preserve the pure felicity
Which home has always given to me;
Let pity touch your soul before
You shove my treasure out the door.
Can your determination be
Averted by my urgent plea
Or act of parliament of senate?
If not, then carry me out in it.

The Secret

*("Academic people in particular are likely to suffer from
the 'Impostor Syndrome.'"—noted psychologist)*

I have a dreadful secret which none of you should tell:
I do not handle praise or approbation very well.
No matter what I've done or I've accomplished in the past,
No matter what the good reviews and clippings I've amassed,
With each succeeding lecture or offering from my pen
I fear that I'm expected then to do it once again.
But there's an unctuous little voice I carry in my head
That whispers, "That was last time. The next time you'll be dead."
And I know that that's the hour when I'll wallow in disgrace,
A farcical disaster with egg upon my face.
I fear that folks will see me then for what I truly am,
A scholarly impostor, a literary sham.
Alas, my friends at last will know and whisper it abroad:
That in the end and after all old Christian is a fraud.
But even then I know that they will look me in the eye,
Will smile at me indulgently and clear their throats—and lie.

A Winter's Tale

(To BJC)

O, for the joys of a winter night,
For the thrill of the pelting sleet
As we draw the strings of our parkas tight
And stamp our frozen feet,
When an icy shell imprisons the trees
And edges the ponds and creeks,
And our blood revives as the keen north breeze
Whets its blade on our cheeks.

O, for the bliss of a night like this,
For the brunt of the winter storm,
But O, for the even greater bliss
Of coming into the warm.
We will thumb our noses at the winds
And laugh at the pounding weather
As we pull our blankets up to our chins
And snuggle up together.

Caveat for the First of March

December is ice and April's green;
March is somewhere in between.
Fierce and brittle? Soft and kind?
She never can make up her mind.
The wise will cast a wary eye
On fleecy clouds and soft blue sky.
But heedless lasses join the boys
To bask in March's tepid joys.

Profs come out of hibernation;
Students plan their spring vacation;
Shoppers hurry yon and hither;
Harried husbands in a dither,
Do the chores their loving wives
Have slyly plotted all their lives.
Peach trees blossom, elm trees leaf,
Doomed, I fear, to frigid grief.

Now bikers from the south and west
On busy streets ride four abreast,
Riders plump and riders slender,
Scorning horn, ignoring fender,
Warmed for now by vernal thaws,
Tomorrow by their Mackinaws.
Beware jogger! Beware sprinter!
On the calendar it's winter.

Spring Song

(To be sung on the Ides of April.)

Winter's over! Welcome spring!
Listen to them grackles sing.
Smell the breezes, warm and sweet,
From the dumpster down the street.
Algae blossoms in the lake,
And tiny creatures yawn and wake,
Each committed in its turn
To make us itch or sting or burn.

Now termites march in single file
To eat our modest domicile;
Once more crab grass in the lawn
Lifts its ugly head at dawn.
Ah, see the pretty fire ant hills
Bursting through like daffodils,
Dirty brown amidst the green.
Quick! Break out the kerosene.

Ballad of I-35

("Caution: Objects in this mirror are nearer

than they appear.")

Father, hear my earnest prayer:
18 wheelers everywhere!
Big behemoths hauling freight
Up and down the Interstate.
Six ahead and eight behind!
Pity mortal humankind.

One in back is creeping nearer,
Filling up in my rear-view mirror,
Tightly clinging to my tail,
Yawning maw like Jonah's whale,
Drooling on my little car
Like a hungry predator.

Now a rig in orange and red
Looms obscenely up ahead:
I clutch my wheel in sheer dismay,
Flying snow-blind in his spray,
Deafened by the dulcet lilt
Of his roaring Peterbilt

Thus I read with little cheer
The sign displayed upon his rear;
While I contemplate surviving
He asks blithely, "How's my driving?"

A View from the Rear

(Confessions of a Church Usher)

On Sundays, if the homily should bore me
I contemplate the sea of heads before me,
Heads of every color and condition—
Black and silver, blonde, brunette and Titian.
You'd need to be as wise as Aristotle
To figure who is real and who is bottle,
Or which coiffeurs spend days on closet shelves.
And bald heads merit study in themselves.
There's one with just a thinness in the rear
And a fellow who is skin from ear to ear,
A few with little "poofs" on either side.
Some seem to sport their hairlessness with pride;
Some comb their few remaining strands across
In effort futile to conceal their loss.
Some heads sit stiff and rigid as a rod;
Some droop in drowsy fellowship with God.
And so we can conclude with due sobriety:
In heads we're blessed with infinite variety.
But as for me, as best I can determine,
I should desist and listen to the sermon.

Tale of a Tooth

Because I am an happy man;
I'll speak the happy truth:
I'm glad to share the news with you
That Eli has a tooth.

It grew when he was very small;
He's had it quite a while.
It's part of Eli's handsome face,
And of his sunny smile.

Yes, Eli's had that tooth before
But now it's loose and wobbly.
Will it fall out, do you suppose,
And leave him snaggled? Probly!

How come that tooth is wiggling loose?
How come he's in a fix?
It's logical and proper
Since Eli's almost six.

Yes, Eli's tooth is wobbly;
It wobbles aft and fore.
I'll bet that wobbly tooth will be
The first of many more.

And in the twinkling of an eye,
When days and weeks have flown,
Before his Grandad knows it
His Eli will be grown.

Song to be Sung by the Wife of a Recently Retired Professor

Now comes the conquering hero home;
He's fought the noble fight.
Henceforth I'll see his earnest face
Morning and noon and night!

When I'm to bed he's hovering near;
When I awake he's there.
How can I get this lovely man
Out of my silver hair?

To smile upon his golden years—
This is my deepest wish,
But some wives' husbands travel
And some wives' husbands fish.

Lord knows he's been a faithful spouse.
I couldn't love him more.
Then why do I have this frantic urge
To shove him out the door?

But this is still my kitchen
And my hands are in the dough.
At least, with Barnes & Noble,
He'll have a place to go.

Visit to the Ophthalmologist

(To RDC)

"Please read the chart upon the door."
"That's easy: F Z B D 4."
"So far so good, but now let's try
The next line with the other eye."
"It starts with Q, or could it be
An O or D or maybe G?"
Then F L C . . ."
"Now try the third."
"I'm sorry but it's sorta blurred."
My aging orbs there's no disguising.
Next time I'll try memorizing.
I've long since bid bi-focals "Bye"
But tell me, what comes after tri—?
I guess its "Onward through the fog!"
Where do I go to get my dog?

RX

I've noted as my hairs grow gray
And as the days go swiftly by
How, while my options seem to fade,
My drug prescriptions multiply:
One for breakfast, three for bed,
Two before the second course,
Pills no bigger than a minute,
Tablets that would choke a horse.

Am I weak or palpitating?
Feeling feverish or chilly?
Got an griping in my belly?
Call for Phiser, Merck or Lilly.
Every ache or creak or groan,
Every red and tender cuticle,
Every cough or sneeze or sniffle
Calls for something pharmaceutical.

The CVS folks are my pals.
I distinctly hear them humming
"Happy days are here again"
Every time they see me coming.

"To tell the truth . . ."

He says, "I always tell it like it is."
These days that seems to be the common buzz.
Well, maybe I would tell it like it is
If ever I knew for sure just what it was.

But bare correctitude is not for me,
I know I'm far too ancient in the tooth
To always deal in stark reality,
Too frosty-haired to always tell the truth.

I'm sometimes grandly awed by people who
Can speak the facts unvarnished to the letter,
But in the grind I've finally reached the view
That truth's OK; but safety! Ah, that's better!"

So when my lovely lady says, "My dear,
I need your judgment and your studied eye.
Does this new outfit emphasize my rear?"
I smile a loving smile and then . . . I lie!

Domesticated or Ballad of the Broken Spirit

When I was a lad and fancy free
I dearly loved, did I,
To lay me down on a blanket roll
And sleep beneath the sky
While the constellations whirled above
And the coyote sang his song,
While the crickets hummed, and
the prairie breeze
Whispered the whole night long.

But then one day I married a maid
Whose spirit was appalled
By the thought of laying her pretty head
Where bugs and beasties crawled.
While I'd reflect on wind and stars
She'd dwell on rats and ticks,
So now we nod to the prairie sky
And head for Motel 6.

The Realist

"Grow old along with me," said Robert Browning,
Then winked and said, "The best is yet to be."
Old Rob, a sober chap, was surely clowning
Or else he wrote when he was twenty-three.

Such counsel smacks of adolescent folly.
He'd not let such opinions pass his lips,
Nor would he be intemperately jolly
If he had my arthritis in his hips.

When arms grow short and stairs are clearly steeper
One quickly starts to feel the autumn blight,
When the fellow who was once a solid sleeper
Must get up every hour of the night.

My take on what they call the golden years
Is just a mite less roseate than his.
With hair on dome replaced by hair in ears
The best is yet to be? Yeah! Sure it is!

But it's my row and I am bound to hoe it
As wallets shrivel and expenses swell.
The ancient seer was wiser than the poet
When he observed, "This getting old is hell!"

Tool Time

"What is it," asks my patient wife,
"With men and hardware stores?"
Whenever she beholds me
Disappearing through the doors.

Some men are slaves to money
And drink makes some men fools;
I fear that I'm addicted
To bolts and clamps and tools.

I'm apt to be a sucker
For anything that's new—
A diesel-powered gimlet,
A counter-clockwise screw,

And once I've bought a drill, a vise,
A tool of any size
It seems to be henceforth
A thing of beauty to my eyes.

When she asks, "Do you need this thing
Still cluttering up the floor?"
I say "Oh, yes! I used it once
In nineteen-ninety-four."

Short Pants

I welcome genial summer in these parts
By suiting out my ample loins in shorts.
I've always tried to figure at my best,
Properly groomed, appropriately dressed,
But being in retirement gets the thanks
For my unblushing liberated shanks.
I love the cooling breezes as they sigh
And circulate around each pudgy thigh,
So shamelessly exposed I leave the house
To dubious opinions from my spouse.

I tell her that I'm going to the mall
To be admired by shoppers one and all,
Baring my calves and ankles as a treat
For all the lovely people that I meet,
And surely as a thrill for womankind.
But she, I fear, is of a different mind.
She's sure that folks will find themselves in stitches
When viewing my abbreviated britches.
So if you chance to cross my pathway, please!
Don't gawk and giggle at my knobby knees.

Love by Degrees

I observe that the world's divided,
If I may be so bold,
Into folks who say, "It's too warm in here,"
And folks who say, "It's too cold."

No matter what the season,
It's always safe to bet
That somebody's got the chill bumps
And somebody's in a sweat.

And so it is, my fair one,
My passion and my delight,
We agree, you see, on so many things
But not on Fahrenheit.

How then shall we live together?
What will we ever do
When your thermostat's set on eighty-nine
And mine's on fifty-two?

We'll let the seasons come and go
And make the most of the weather.
If we freeze, let's freeze to each other;
If we melt, let's melt together.
(In tribute to the incomparable O.N.)

"No Doggy Bags, Please!"

(A lament over the passing of the Piccadilly)

My Frau and I discover with surprise
And with a certain measure of dismay
The cafeterias we patronize
Have gone "kaput" or else they've gone "buffet."

No more three veggies and a glass of tea,
No due restraint when we go out to dine,
No circumspection at a modest fee,
But "all you can eat for seven ninety-nine."

You in the know please tell me on the level,
Am I in deadly peril for my soul,
And are these merchants agents of the Devil,
Sworn to subvert my shaky self control?

I recognize temptation a la carte;
I'm sure that I'll be helpless to defeat it.
I'm really not a glutton in my heart,
I'm just too cheap to pay and not to eat it.

I know I'll rue the folly of my ways;
I fear my diet is lost beyond recall,
So here's a toast to overflowing trays,
Good fellowship and bad cholesterol.

Reflections on Aging

"Face it, "he said, "You're over the hill."
So runs the old cliché.
But if that's true then shouldn't it be
Downhill the rest of the way?

Shouldn't the load seem lighter now?
Softer the southern breezes?
Shouldn't the roadside daisies bloom
Without kachoos and wheezes?

The sun grows hotter on my brow,
The ruts are surely deeper,
And the hill they say I've finally topped
Just keeps on getting steeper.

I haven't faced a downhill slope
Since Rover was a pup.
You never make it over the hill;
It just keeps going up.

Grouch

I woke up feeling cross the other morning.
There really wasn't any reason why.
No bellyache had disarrayed my slumber,
No red and stuffy nose, no bloodshot eye.

I snarled at the cheery TV person,
Scowled in the mirror, grumbled at the cat.
I mumbled as I read the op-ed pages
And told my spouse that she was getting fat.

From time to time I think that I'm entitled
Thus to try stranger, neighbor, child or wife
As one who now these many, many seasons
Has suffered the indignities of life.

The only thing to do is to indulge me
Till I improve. My friends and family know
To smile and to ignore this grumpy person,
And I'll be sweet in just an hour or so.

Insomnia

11:00 p.m.: I've really got to hit the hay;
Tomorrow is a busy day.
I'll clear my teeming mind until
Repose can claim me as it will.

1200 a.m.: That didn't work! For heaven's sake,
I think I'm even more awake.
I'll work a puzzle or I'll read.
Six hours is all I really need.

1:00 a.m.: Come on, I've got to get some sleep!
There's little use in counting sheep.
What soporific can I number
To lull my brain to peaceful slumber?

2:OO a.m.: No use! The chance for sleep is gone.
I'll never close my eyes till dawn.
I guess I'll fold my hands and wait
And patiently . . . accept . . . my . . .

Coffee at Burger King

We're there each Monday regular as dawn
Before the week is properly begun
To thaw our creaky joints and then to yawn
And bask together in the morning sun.

A band of craggy fossils, worn and gray,
In out-sized sweats or dingy dungarees
Hoping for just an hour to hold at bay
Old age that creeps upon us by degrees.

There's Dick, so cold of frame and warm of heart,
And Bill, sly as a fox but always kind,
And Tom, who's IQ must be off the chart
And—Let me see now. Who else comes to mind?

A John or two, a Jim, another Bill,
Alan and Chuck, all blithe and nimble-witted—
Loren, with his biscuit from the grill.
That can't be all. Now, whom have I omitted?

Ah, what a cadre! Never did the fates
Give ancient Athens such a troupe of sages.
I'm sure we hold within our frosty pates
Between us all the wisdom of the ages.

Tail Lights

December 1

The happy news is in! They'll all be here,
To fill our Christmas holidays with cheer:
Elizabeth from college in the East—
She's oldest. And Ella—she's the least.
She's walking now! And Savvy, with those eyes,
And Sidney, manic whirlwind in disguise,
And Eli, our grandson solitaire,
With joy enough for all of us to share,
Together with assorted children four
Who bore them and will bear them here once more.

January 1

The news is in! They're going home at last.
The days of Christmastide are slipping past.
With countless games of ball and stories told,
The Yule and I are quickly growing old,
And as we age, the truth is clear: Old Dad
No longer has the energy he had.
With arms about my neck and tear in eye
I hug them one more time and say goodbye.
I'll miss the little scamps, but truth to tell
I think I'll bear the parting rather well.

After festive days there is no sight
Sweeter than tail lights fading in the night.

Mutt!

I watch the dog shows on TV
Where pure-breds preen and strut.
When asked, "What kind of dog is yours?"
I smile and say, "A Mutt!"

My brother has a dachshund,
My neighbor has a lab,
But next to my dog Nipper
They're colorless and drab.

A colleague paid a bundle
For his pure-bred Papillon
But they never let her roam the yard
Or chew upon a bone.

Another neighbor loves to brag
Of his noble Irish setter.
Now, I'm sure his dog is very well
But my little mutt is better.

I often call him, "Boy dog!"
That's really not his name,
But whether that or something else
He loves me just the same.

I'll tell you why my Nipper
Is worthy of his feed!
His shaggy little frame combines
The best of every breed.

A Wry Retrospective

When I was a boy my elders all advised,
"Hard work and virtue, Lad: These are the way!
Be good and keep your shoulder to the wheel.
You'll be rewarded on that future day."

If ever I held this sage advice in doubt,
If ever I thought their council overblown,
They'd nod their noggins knowingly and say,
"You'll understand it all when you are grown."

"Behave yourself and always do your best!
Shirk not your duties and you'll gain the gold!"
But when I labored all I got was tired.
When I got older all I got was old.

I've tried to be a good boy all my life,
But if I got the chance to do it twice,
Perhaps I'd be more cautious in my virtue;
Perhaps I'd be more joyful in my vice.

Two postulates I've garnered from the years,
And neither truth should come as a surprise:
Working harder doesn't make you rich!
Growing older doesn't make you wise!

Decisions

"Where would you like to go for dinner, dear?"
"It doesn't matter. Anywhere you say."
"How 'bout the China Grill?"
"That's fine with me."
"Or maybe Luby's?"
"That would be OK."

"The Cotton Patch? Or Applebee's?"
"That's fine."
"No, really, Sweetheart, this one is your call.
"Is it Outback or Smokey Bones? Decide!"
"Whatever, dearest. I don't care at all."
. . . .
"An after dinner stroll up through the Mall?
Or is it Target you prefer?"
"Sounds good."
"Or maybe Barnes & Noble for a while?
Or Books-a-million?"
"If you think we should."
. . . .
"What would you like for breakfast?"
"I don't care."
"What about eggs?"
"That's fine."
"Scrambled? Fried?"
"Yes, fried or scrambled. Either would be good."

"A a a a a a a a a a a a a a a a a a a a h!!!!"

"Aw, judge! You know it's justified homicide."

Dominoes

I've always tried to emulate
My father and my mother:
Their kindness and their humor,
Their devotion to each other,

But the nearest that those gentle folk
Would ever come to war
Was when they'd take the dominoes
Out of the dresser drawer.

My father was as gracious
As anyone could choose,
But when it came to dominoes
He didn't like to lose.

When Daddy triumphed it was skill
Or strategy he'd planned,
But it was always luck, you see,
When Mama won a hand.

I'd note the twinkle in her eye
She scarcely could contain
As she'd send him to the boneyard
To grumble and complain.

"My gosh!" he'd say, "Another trey!
Pure horseshoes! Goodness knows,
If you fell into the sewer you'd come up
Smelling like a rose."

I'd smile upon these joustings for
When all was said and done
I knew from the beginning
That I was the lucky one.

Bammaw

(to JP with love)

Friends we had been for lo, these many seasons
But friends we were upon a lengthy tether.
Uncommon the occasions when we'd meet,
That is, until our children got together.

They spoke and smiled and then their troth was plighted,
And so, as is the way with love and nature,
We found ourselves confronting the dilemma
Of proper grandparental nomenclature.

I would be "Grandad,"—simple, crisp and done!
On this fair truth there must be little doubt,
But how were Eli and Ella Josephine
To sort two frosty coiffured ladies out?

Little enough there is that's fair and clear
In this perplexing universe, and so
It was decreed: Memaw is on Bellaire
And Bammaw it is who lives on Charbonneau.

Bammaw, of the soft, disarming chuckle,
Witty and sly but generous to a flaw,
And when our children come another bedroom!
The gal we call our "mother-in-law-in-law."

Inventory

Egad! Another birthday has come skittering 'round the block
And what's the use of natal day if not for taking stock?
So here I stand at early dawn in all my naked glory.
I groan a bit but I admit it's time for inventory.

The act of self-analysis is not without its pain
But I shall try to judge what's truly loss and what is gain.
I'll shake my early-morning head and clear my stuffy sinuses
And calculate as best I can the plusses and the minuses.

My hair absconded years ago. I scarcely know it's gone,
But I have gained another face that once it grew upon.
I have an extra pound or two and joints that often creak
But I always get them going by the middle of the week.

My gall bladder's left me; it vanished long ago
And over many decades I've lost a tooth or so,
But of my other gear and sundry parts with which I started
I'm proud to say that none of them has surgically departed.

The hair now grows within my ears. My toenails are a sight.
I doze off during sermon time and lie awake at night,
But by way of compensation, I'm sure my wife will say
That my attitude grows sweeter with every passing day.

Despite my many flaws for which I need to make amends
I'm greatly rich in grandkids and doubly blessed with friends.
And as I launch another year and teeter on the brink
My greatest consolation is: I've kept my wits—I think!

Second Banana

I think it's always been my fate to be
In youth, at age and everywhere between
Responding to some other captaincy—
Parent, chairman, president or dean.

'Tis always thus for mortal folks like me
To bow the knee to heroes, knights and kings.
My kind with wily Cassius must agree
The fault's our own that we are underlings.

But I'll not envy him who runs the show.
I'm sure the snow-capped mountaintop is grand.
Still, I'm contented just a rung below.
I make a decent second-in-command,

Just ask the one who's truly fit to see
How I have kept my true and proper station,
Modestly serving fifty years and three
Under the Betty Jean administration.

Button

My shirt has an extra button without a buttonhole,
Which is needed for the button to fulfill its proper role.
It's not required at present; it's down below my waist
And when the shirt is buttoned it's lonely and displaced.

But I'm grateful for my button; to its pearly gloss I cling
For in these times I treasure an extra anything.
Like a belt worn with suspenders or a chain upon the door
It's sometimes nice to bank upon a little something more.

Remember days of long ago when for a song and dance
You'd buy a suit and you'd receive an extra pair of pants?
And once a baker's dozen meant a bonus loaf or bun.
I'm lucky now to get an even twelve before I'm done.

Nothing else I buy these days provides me with a spare,
So it's very reassuring to know my button's there.
Thus though the powers of Kismet may against me be arrayed,
If I should lose a button, I think I've got it made.

A Higher Calling

I've spent my lifetime singing in the choir.
I started as a cherub-faced beginner,
But puberty then raised its urgent head
And I made the move from treble up to tenor.

For this I thank the Lord and DNA.
We tenors are a choice and fancy breed,
The shining silver trumpets of the choir,
The musical aristocrats indeed.

Pity the basses on the other end,
Poor hapless fellows, not as blessed by half,
Doomed all their singing days to growling air
An octave or two below the staff.

I always treat them gently when I can.
I've tried to be as gracious as you please,
But I'm sure that these poor, harmonic drudges
Are jealous of my A flats and my Gs.

One day, when I stand before my judge
As he wisely disposes saint and sinner,
He'll wink at me and whisper, "Come on in!
We're always glad to have another tenor."

Facts are Facts

(Same song, second verse)

I think I've said it once before:
My love's a sleepy head;
When twilight steals across the sky
Her thoughts are for her bed.

While me, I am a night owl;
I prize the witching time
For Mozart or for Shakespeare
Or to worry with a rhyme.

I need those priceless hours
To resupply my cup.
Her ten o'clock's for winding down;
Mine's for revving up.

Once, when I saw her start to nod,
I pleaded, with a smile,
"Let's play some Hearts or Dirty Eight;
Stay up with me a while."

"Our bodies are different!" she complained.
I grinned a grin: "My pet,
I noticed that delightful fact
The moment that we met."

"Our bodies," my love, are different—
That's a fact beyond debate!
If they were the same I never would
Have asked you for a date."

Frustration

"Tear here!" it clearly says upon the tag;
"Push up!" it reads upon the bottle cap.
I tear and rip the bottom from the bag;
I push and dump the tablets in my lap.

Or wrestle till my fingertips are peeled
And struggle till I sink into despair
On packages designed never to yield
To earnest effort, blandishments or prayer.

I weep a tear when all my efforts fizzle;
I hurl the stubborn package at the wall;
I go in search of blow torch, axe or chisel
And curse the fellow who began it all.

I'm sure somewhere in Dante's purgatory
He'll stand with flames and tongues of lava lapping,
And over him a sign will tell the story:
"The fellow who invented blister wrapping."

Early Bird

Since I was just a little guy
It's always been my fate
To be the one that's early
When the world is running late.

For every hour I've waited
On others of my species
If I had just a nickel
I would be as rich as Croesus.

I show up at the starting gate;
The morning sky is red,
But the fellow with the starting gun
Is still asleep in bed.

It's been the story of my life—
It's true beyond debate!—
To play the game of "twiddlethumbs,"
To hurry up and wait.

It isn't that I'm insecure
Or anything like that.
I just don't want to fool around
And miss my time at bat.

I'm sure I'll hear when I appear
At heaven's golden gate:
"Please wait a thousand years or so;
St, Peter's running late."

Rip Van Betty

I asked, when we were courtin',
If she would like to go
Uptown to the Majestic
For a movin' pichur show.

I bought her buttered popcorn.
I charmed her with my wit
And after the show I treated her
To a banana split.

In my fevered brain I wondered
If I should take the leap,
But as I drove her home that night
My love went fast asleep.

I looked at my sleeping beauty
And quietly blew my lid.
"I'll never call that girl again!"
But, happily, I did.

And now she lies beside me
Lost in a pleasant dream,
While me? I count the hours
Like the ripples on the stream.

I say, "Sweetheart, you have slumbered
More than fifty years away."
"A clear conscience," she snickers.
"An empty head," I say.

Smile When You Say That, Podner!

On sultry summer weekends
I'd often make my way
Up to the Bison Theater
For the Saturday matinee.

Deep in my britches pocket
Were nickels enough, I knew,
For a western double feature
And a tootsie roll or two.

The hero's hat was always white
And the villain dressed in black,
And only a craven coward shot
A fellow in the back.

And my restless soul was reassured,
When all was said and done,
That evil always got it due
And virtue always won.

I'd hiss the devious banker
With the gold watch in his vest
And cheer the guy who proudly wore
The star upon his chest.

But one thing I never understood,
As nature took its course,
With the rancher's daughter standing there,
Why would he kiss the horse?

Season to Taste

I've got to cook a pot-roast for the family and a guest,
So I'll try some online recipes to see what they suggest.
This one calls for Cayenne, oregano and cumin.
To me that sounds too pungent for professor or for human.

Here's one that says to add some cloves and marinate in beer.
Sure! I can see yours truly with a six-pack standing near.
This one pumps for celery seed and that one praises curry—
So many different recipes my eyes are getting blurry.

There's Nutmeg and there's bay leaves, there's Marjoram
　　　　and there's sage—
I'd name the other spices but I have to turn the page—
Or mustard seed or turmeric or lemon juice or lime.
I'd like to try them all but I haven't got the thyme.

My rule concerning flavor is—if ever I'm in doubt—
"I can always add more spices; I can never take them out."
But with this rich abundance I can't begin to cope
So I'll throw it in the Crockpot and season it with hope.

The Difference

If you're up on genes and chromosomes
It isn't a surprise
That girls have double-Xs
And boys have X and Ys.

I wish that information
Had never reached my wife
Or my two clever daughters
Who illuminate my life.

For when I get cross or difficult
I see them wink and grin
And whisper, "He can't help it;
It's that tedious Y again."

When my lively grandson visits
And I hear his thud and thump
My daughter says with eyebrows raised,
"Ys like to make things jump."

The world would be a better place,
They say with twinkling eyes,
If the double Xs were in charge
And not a bunch of Ys.

Now, whether from Norway or Brazil,
From Timbuktu or Texas,
I grant a difference between
Us Y's and double Xs

But I smile a smile and bear with grace
The jokes at my expense,
For I think the Frenchman has it right:
"Vive le difference!"

The Rules of Life

(Murphy's Law: If anything can go wrong, it will.)

Though years have hastened, no one's found a flaw
In the searing truth of Murphy's famous law.
But from it many rules and maxims flow
To guide our mortal struggle here below.

For instance, I'm sure you'll understand
That "Everything takes longer than you planned."
And here's a truth—I would not dare to fudge it—
"Nothing gets done on schedule or in budget."

A solemn rule we all should take to heart
Is that, "Everything sooner or later falls apart."
And as we age we take the bitter pill
That, "If one thing doesn't go, another will."

Another faithful rule, if you'll but heed it:
"As soon as you discard a thing you need it."
Nor will you find this caveat in books:
"Nothing is quite as easy as it looks."

There's many a sober axiom or rule
Our teachers never taught to us in school.
But many years of living life, they say,
Will cure of us all youth's naiveté.

Should this depressing litany of laws
Banish your blissful mood and give you pause,
Do not despair; I have one maxim more:
"Take heart, because you can't fall off the floor."

Lines Written in the Morning Twilight at 6:00 AM (DST)

(To SCB)

Here in my lair the shadows hang
Like moss upon the walls;
Outside my window traffic hums
And sober duty calls.
That selfsame duty bids me leave
The comfort of my room,
Gird up my sleepy loins and then
Press onward through the gloom.

If the affairs of mice and men
Were put within my power,
I'd fix the launching of the day
At some more decent hour.
Oh, what a burden to the flesh,
What anguish for the soul
To be a night-owl in a world
Where larks are in control.

Get Away from Me!

One day of late—I don't know how—
I managed something truly dumb
While out in my garage, and now
I have a black and purple thumb.

Do I exaggerate? I know
I shouldn't take it so to heart,
But every object here below
Seems sworn to bump my wounded part.

The slightest touch from foe or friend
Can quickly send me to my knees.
It matters not what you intend,
So kindly keep your distance please.

To some secluded spot I'll flee
Where I can bellyache and grouch
And spare my sad extremity
From this encroaching univ—OUCH!!!

Message for Our Answering Machine

To all our friends and kindred: Smile!
You've reached the Christian domicile.
We can't pick up the phone just now.
Perhaps were in a family row.
Perhaps we're busy or away;
Perhaps we've had a dreadful day;
Perhaps we're in the tub, or worse—
Fighting Montezuma's curse
Or sitting underneath the trees—
Haven't we had a lovely breeze?
But which of us would dare complain
If we could get an inch of rain?
My lawn's a dismal shade of beige,
My weeds are in their final stage,
And ah! If you could only see
My desperate liriope.

  So leave a word. Or better yet,
Just drop in for a tête-à-tête.
Forget the e-mail and the fax;
Come by for lemonade and snacks.
You're keeping busy? And, I'd guess,
You've missed the flu.—But I digress!

  As I was saying, "At the 'ding'
Tell the recorder anything
That you would like for us to know
And we'll get" . . . Click! Hello! Hello!

Dog in a Fix

Our pooch went to the vet last week.
Since home to us he came
He's had to wear about his head
The plastic "Cone of Shame."

No other way, you see, because
That darned incision itches.
It's either be a "cone-head"
Or pull out all his stitches.

We gamely struggle not to smile
Since he's been forced to don it,
For he's the very image of
Aunt Sally in her bonnet.

I'm sure his canine ego
Is wounded to the core
To endure the hoots and snickers
Of the dogs who live next door:

"Well, Hi there, Mother Hubbard!
How sweet you look today.
Go give your dog his morning bone
And let him out to play."

He looks at me with grieving eyes.
I hear his doleful plea!
"I've tried to be a good dog; why
Have you done this to me?"

Ode on Forty-Eight Years Married to The Same Woman, and Glad of it

To all my friends I now concede:
In our fifty-near flirtation
Her love has been an endless deed
Of supererogation.

Let cynics hurl their snide attacks!
Let misanthrope's disparage!
We're here to scratch each other's backs—
Excuse enough for marriage!

Heron

So there I sat, as silent as a stone,
Watching my cork caress the quiet ripples
On the April pond,
When he came stalking (storking?) in the shallows.
Past the crumbling jetty,
Past the mud flat and the broken clamshells,
Around the cat-tails at the margin,
Peering singly at the murky water,
Lurching as he walked,
Like Ichabod Crane,
Hands clasped behind him as he paced.
Suddenly, as swift as thought, he speared
The crappie I had fixed my hopes upon.
I watched it wriggle down his serpent neck.
He fixed a mocking yellow eye on me,
Said "Gronk" and flew away.

Girls

Since I was a lad and first discovered girls
I've counted it a privilege and a joy
That I was planned and properly designed
And sent into the world to be a boy.

From early on my ardent soul would fancy
Each pretty face or figure that I met,
And I would sigh in homage to the grace
Of every blonde, each redhead, each brunette.

Soprano? Alto?—didn't really matter!
To any friend or casual inquirer
I'd cheerfully confess myself to be
An equal opportunity admirer.

For a fellow of my exquisite discernment
I reckoned it to be my solemn duty
To honor every lovely lass I'd meet
With heartfelt thoughts in praise of love and beauty.

One day I met the beauty of them all.
She smiled that special smile to me, and then,
When she became my one and only, I
Became the most monogamous of men.

But then she said to me one sunny morning,
As in our breakfast nook we snugly sat,
"You never notice girls, I'm sure, my darling."
I smiled: "I wouldn't go as far as that!

Sweet Music

"You're easier to live with," so says my worthy spouse,
"When you've found yourself a project to create around the house."
She's right, of course. I've spent my life upon the people track
And it's nice to greet a piece of wood that doesn't argue back.

But oh, the conversations we have when we're alone!
And every woody species has a psyche of its own.
There's pine, fresh-faced and honest, brought newly from the mill
And dramatic Cocobolo from the forests of Brazil.

My basswood is mild-mannered, cooperative and plain,
But my brash mesquite's flamboyant, a fandango in its grain.
There's walnut, rich and sober, and zebrawood exotic;
There's graceful ash, and balsa wood, unstable and neurotic.

There's sturdy fir—a trifle bland—and rosewood charismatic,
And mild plebian sycamore and oak aristocratic,
And redwood, tough and durable, immune to nasty weather,
And willow and olive wood, all in the bin together.

There's birch, upright and versatile, and poplar, always game,
And half—a-dozen other friendly species I could name,
So pass my cherrywood baton and sander down to me
And together we will all strike up a woodland symphony.

Limericks for People with Taste

On Limericks

Some limericks are gentle and lyrical;
Some limericks are sharp and satirical;
*   Some are laden with spleen,*
*   Some dyspeptic and mean,*
But a limerick that's clean—that's a miracle.

Prayer

If our folly elicits a sigh
From your merciful Lordship on high,
*   The dastardly rumor*
*   You've no sense of humor*
One look at ourselves puts to lie.

Some will judge as unworthy and vile
Our flippant, unmannerly style.
*   Though it may be unfit,*
*   Our irreverent wit*
Please accept with a pardoning smile.

On Miracles

A brown and white Spaniel named Ferd
Flapped his ears and took off like a bird.
*   When asked if he knew*
*   That dogs never flew*
He said, "No, it just never occurred."

The Wild Party

At a party a lady named Byrd
Sidled up to her husband and purred:
"My dearest, I think
You've had too much to drink.
You're getting a little bit blurred."

Dougal McDougal

Said a bugler named Dougal McDougal,
When asked to perform on his bugle:
"A fanfare, I'd guess,
Would never impress,
But perhaps a Bach prelude and fugue'll."

The Critic

An elegant gourmet named Dewey
At a dinner was served ratatouille.
He leaned over the tray
And sniffed the bouquet
And uttered the expletive, "Phooey!"

Egghead

A fair Mensa member named Tresch
Has an outlook both novel and fresh.
Says she, "I like chess
But I find that it's less
Entertaining than sins of the flesh.

Frenzy

A fragile professor named Burke
When his sophomores drove him berserk,
Called a feminist "Dearie,"
Denied Einstein's theory
And blasphemed Allah to a Turk.

Cap and Gown

A pale Academic named Keys
Has a Masters and six Ph.Ds.
Remarked his physician,
"As to your condition,
You're killing yourself by degrees."

The Mathematician

To Pythagorus wise a salute!
His theory's really a beaut
    On the use and abuses
    Of hypotenuses
And angles obtuse and acute.

But I'd like to inquire, if I might:
What are the two sides in this fight?
    What's the root of a square
    And does anyone care
If a triangle's wrong or it's right?

Loch Ness

A lovely young lady named Bess
Went swimming in murky Loch Ness,
    Which is twenty miles plus
    From the station by bus
And . . . Forgive me! I fear I digress.

Myopia

An astronomer royal named Maury
With a blush and a grimace said, "Sorry!"
    To a firefly who flew
    Through his angle of view.
"I thought you were Alpha Centauri."

Revelation

Said a silly inventor named Spruell,
Who fashioned a two-legged stool
*   And sat thereupon,*
*   "Ah, the truth starts to dawn;*
I perceive now that I am a fool."

Ecstasy

A silly young lady named Bickler
Just loved to have gentlemen tickler;
*   She would giggle and coo,*
*   Then cry out, "Mon dieu"*
And shoot up in the air perpendickler.

Under the Big Top

The great human cannonball, Sven,
Missed the net and at last cashed it in.
*   I doubt that we can*
*   Hold out hope for a man*
Of his caliber ever again.

The Purist

A grammar fanatic named Groom
Plunged forty-nine feet to his doom
From a perilous perch
In a towering birch
While teaching an owl to say, "Whom."

Little Big Horn

Said Custer, as two thousand Sioux
In war-paint jumped up and said "Bioux!"
"When history is written
They'll say that I've bitten
Off more than I'm able to chioux."

Bad Day on Mt. Moriah
(Genesis 22)

Isaac sighed, "What a day this has been!
I barely escaped with my skin.
But one thing I know:
I'll be darned if I go
Out camping with Papa again."

Online

A weary saleslady named Baxter
Found that traveling harried and taxed her.
So she dieted, and then,
When she grew very thin
She lay down on the desk and they faxed her.

9-1-1

A deplorable sinner from Kent
Encrusted his dog with cement.
While folks east and west
Lifted voice in protest,
The dog could but mumble, "Repent."

The Shrink

Said Freud, "I've invented analysis
For folk's psychic bunions and calluses.
When I pry up their lids
They'll discover their Ids
Full of March Hares, Mad Hatters and Alices.

Isaac and the Apple

Said Sir Isaac, with ominous air,
"I've a theory I feel I must share
About Nature's laws,
But I'm Solemn because
Of the gravity of the affair."

A Greeting to New Faculty

(Written in fifteen minutes for professor daughter Suzii to use at
faculty orientation.)

We welcome you all with this thought:
The battle remains to be fought.
We commend to you duly
Your students unruly
And colleagues beset and distraught.

Reflections on Ice-breaking

A daring young man from Green Bay
Took a ride on the lake in a sleigh.
But the ice was too thin.
Tell his nearest of kin
That his last words were "Anchors aweigh!"

Revelation II

A prudish old maiden named Tiffani
Underwent an erotic epiphany
    Which she said, "I declare,
    I shall certainly share
With all future paramours, iffani."

Disclaimer

As now I look back and reflect
On these verses and start to suspect
    That the little of mind
    Are likely to find
Them politically less than correct.

I deny—though the rumors be rife—
Ever writing such stuff in my life.
    These were found in my lap
    When I woke from a nap
And were written, I think, by my wife.

Animalimericks for Elizabeth and Other Very Intelligent Children

The Vulture

The vulture's a grim apparition
With appetite gross. In addition,
His manners are crummy,
And if he gets chummy
Please check with your family physician.

The Kiwi

The Kiwi's an odd little thing
With scarcely a feather or wing,
And this, for a bird,
Is pretty absurd,
So it never flies north in the spring.

The Toad

In May you'll perhaps see the toad
On your lawn when it's sprinkled and mowed.
He's a singer in June
By the light of the moon.
In July he's a spot on the road.

Tyrannosaurus Rex

Now relax, child, and stifle your fears!
T. Rex isn't what he appears;
*   This monster colossal*
*   Is only a fossil*
And has been for millions of years.

The Amoeba

This miniature animal who
Lives down in the muck and the goo
*   Is a single cell only,*
*   But if he gets lonely*
He promptly divides into two.
(Is that something you think you could do?)

The Tortle

I believe that the tortoise is found
On the desert and other dry ground,
*   While turtles are livers*
*   In oceans and rivers.*
(Or is it the other way 'round?)

Old Photograph

Where has it been these decades, tucked away
In a faded envelope within a box
Or deftly hidden from the light of day
Behind the worn-out underwear and socks?
So there we sit—some unremembered place:
The pretty girl in deep blue dungarees,
Her dark hair luminous about her face,
The checkered blouse, her arms around her knees.
And younger much than I can now recall:
The slender youth who wears the silly grin,
So sure, beside her there against the wall,
That fate had him the happiest of men.
And on the back, scrolled by an unknown pen,
"1/26 in '52"—Come spring,
As the firewheel and the phlox were coming in
She'd smile to him that smile and take his ring.

Three Love Songs

Autumn Spring

We have been older, dear, than we are now
And did not see the coming of the spring,
Receive it with such willing, or allow
The whispered truth in every blossoming.
But are we not more ready to be love
One to the other, and to hold the splendor
Of twilight, and of this soft shower above?
Our passions are not poorer, but more tender.
We are with heavy time less weighted now—
Not less attuned to April's haunting pain
But, apt with quieter spirits, we endow
With joy the gentle falling of the rain.
How pleasant to be innocent again!

On Fifty Years Together

(August 9, 2002)

In August, when I hear the curlew's cry
And once again become a vagabond,
Fixed on the shifting patterns of the sky,
The sun-drenched prairies and the hills beyond,
When I lament the odysseys that failed
And, on this latter shore, are surely lost,
Why does it seem that I have ever sailed
Hull-down to fair horizons never crossed?
But I will claim these decades roundly spent,
Closed gladly in to home and time and place,
Wistful of vagrant skies and yet content,
My universe defined by your embrace.
One pole star in changing heavens I've found:
I was not free until my heart was bound.

To my Love

(August 9, 1952-August 9, 2007)

As I woke at early dawn,
Some rendezvous to keep,
Beside me there, my love, I caught you
Smiling in your sleep.

In dreams, I knew, your fancy
Would be fetterless and free
But reckoned in my vanity
The smile was meant for me.

I thought, as you lay sleeping
On our well-worn marriage bed,
Of the hours when I've found that look
Dearer to me than bread,

The smile you've smiled to me in spring
And in October's haze
For nineteen thousand seven hundred
Three and twenty days.

Six "Elizabethan" Songs

Déjà vu

(To my daughter's daughter)

Bright as any April hour,
Newly minted April flower,
Smiles and tears succinctly mated,
Music gently modulated,
Cheek as soft as woodland rabbit,
Gossamer your April habit.
Lilting! Laughing! Ere she grew
There was once a girl like you.

Wind Song

(A Matin)

At dawn a frisky yearling breeze
Jostled awake the sleeping trees.
The cottonwood by the meadow race
Fluttered her skirts to the winds embrace,
While deep in the shadowy wood, the oak
And the silver ash and the elm tree woke,
And, stretching their drowsy branches high,
Gave a creaky salute to the morning sky.
The sycamore tree and the feathery willow
Called as you slept upon your pillow,
"Awake! Awake to this fragrant dawn,
And soon, or the April hour is gone."
"Come out, sweet child," I heard them say,
"And dance your dance to the breaking day,"
And the new leaves whispered with every breath,
"Elizabeth! Elizabeth!"

Lullaby for Elizabeth

Venus hangs bright in the moon's silver bow,
Darkness lies snug on the warm meadow's breast,
Swaddling in shadows the wee things that go
Soft in the whispering grasses below
To slumber and rest.

The song of the nightbird dissolves in the air
And gently distills on the hill's burly crest.
Like dust from an angel's wing glistening there,
It sifts through your window and sprinkles your hair.
Little girl, rest.

Over your crib in the velvety dome
Where countless star children are hurrying west,
Bright Vega is calling her babies to come
As her ebony petticoats gather them home.
Dearest one, rest.

Vision by Sunlight

(Elizabeth at Two)

What else is grace, of all sweet gracious things,
But happiness upon a summer hill,
Held captive by the swallow's flashing wings,
Constrained by mirth to do the summer's will,
And quick to each transparent shadow racing
The bright, scudding clouds toward heaven's end,
Reaching eager hands, as if embracing
The finest joy: to laugh against the wind.

Magic

(To Elizabeth on her third birthday)

Happy enchantress,
Practitioner of ancient arts unlearned
From Prospero's drowned book,
Yours is the magic of gentle Ariel,
Untouched by spite,
Gold-flecked from splitting sunbeams in your flight,
Diaphanous as rainbowed mists
That vanish in the airs of bright and endless springs.
From what lost deep and by what runic art
Do you call up such music to cajole
The Caliban within my soul,
To do such wonder-working in my heart?

Eyes

The forest is full of eyes;
They watch as we wander through;
They are bright in the purple shadows
And soft from the evening dew.
They glow like coals in the gloaming
From the deepening red of the skies,
And now, in the dark, the meadows too
Are lit with a thousand eyes.
They see your eyes in the darkness
And ask you not to depart.
The world has a way with eyes, child,
And with a grandfather's heart.

The Roadside Fire

(To DBH)

When I was a lad I had a friend
And we shared a manly love,
And we joyed, we two, in the road beneath
And the arching sky above.

At day's bright end we'd turn aside
And sit on our trekker's load
As we dreamed our dreams in the shadows
Of our fire beside the road.

We'd bid farewell to the setting sun
And watch as the stars came through,
And we knew that the world was well and good
And our comradeship was true.

But then one day he loved a maid,
And I did the same, you see,
And his became his very heart
And mine was the soul of me.

But still, when I see a winding road
As I watch the dusk expire,
I think I see his wistful face
In the blush of the roadside fire.

(In appreciation to RLS)

Three Songs for Christmastide

Vigil

O, let us keep vigil
Here, among the stars,
Here, where the winds sigh softly
And the distant horizon glows
With lanterns and with candles.

Let us keep vigil in the darkness,
In the comforting darkness,
For darkness becomes mystery.
It is the true milieu of God,

Let us keep vigil,
With our senses honed
To the night sounds about us.
This is the night that
Annuls the rush of time.
Listen: the wail of labor,
The mewl of life aborning.
Let us keep vigil;
It is the night of nights.
(For Christmas Eve)

C. W. Christian

Eve of Nativity

The Christ Candle is burning;
The hour draws near;
The stillness of the watchful night
Comes on us.
Hush! No idle words!
No tinkling sound of temple or bazaar!
Only rapt silence!
Only the pregnant plenitude of mystery!
We stand with open mouths.
We cannot fathom how:
The Word again is flesh
And dwells among us.

     (For Christmas Eve)

Daybreak

. . . And when the morning came
And the Judean sunlight warmed the stable
And the shepherds went their way
Back to the hunching hills and to their sheep
And the weary father rubbed his eyes,
Cast one more loving look
Upon the sleeping mother and her baby
And slept as well,
A child came shyly
And peered into the stable,
Fragrant with hay and the earthiness of life.
She looked into the faces of the sleeping family.
She stood for a moment
Over the small, round visage
In the cattle trough.
She kissed the holy child
And stole away.
            (For Christmas Morning)

The Man Who Hated Christmas

John Bickle hated Christmas.
He declared it could do without him.
It wasn't just a passing whim.
Once you beheld him, stiff and grim,
You really couldn't doubt him.
He never glowed with Yuletide joy
Or gave a pretty gift or toy
To any little girl or boy
Or anyone about him.

He never dressed his modest cot
With garlands or a wreath,
Never a sprig of mistletoe
For friends to stand beneath.
He snorted when the folks came forth
In holiday apparel
And never was his spirit stirred
By greetings or a jolly word.
He muttered when he overheard
A wassail or a carol.

And then one Christmas Eve there came
A knock upon his door!
He found his neighbor's tiny child
He'd sometimes seen before.
She, balancing upon her toes
And smiling—What do you suppose?
She stretched up to her very height
And in the fading Yuletide light,
While one great star was shining bright,
She kissed him—on his nose.

He saw her eyes, which glittered
Like the heavens overhead;
She laid a cookie in his hand
And silently, she fled.
Then, to John Bickle's vast surprise,
A teardrop he could not disguise
Brightened his sad and bleary eyes.
"My, my, What's this?" he said.

He snuffed and sniffled; then he wiped
That tear upon his sleeve.
"Hurrump," he said, "This frigid air!
That's it, I do believe!"
But, rooted on that very spot,
He smiled and muttered, "Maybe not!"
How could I ever have forgot?
Tonight is Christmas Eve."

He stood at his chamber window.
The bells of the brown church tower
Rang out "Adeste Fidelis"
As they marked the passing hour.
He smiled at the bright church windows
With candles flickering through
And the children singing down below.
"Why do I love Christmas so?"
Said John, "I'm sure that I don't know.
I only know I do."

With a nod to A. A. Milne

L'envoi

Great Mozart had octaves and thirds
And Audubon pigments and birds.
 The lark has his trill
  To enchant and to thrill.
The poet has only his words.

These poems, whether noble or vile,
Are yours without humbug or guile.
 If the form be unfit
  And feeble the wit,
Please accept with a wink and a smile.

CPSIA information can be obtained at www.ICGtesting.com
Printed in the USA
LVOW07s0220160216

475257LV00004BA/275/P